孔子

Heroes and Role Models | Non-Fiction Series

Copyright © 2022 by Level Learning, INC. and Washington Yu Ying PCS™
Original and Edited Text Copyright © 2022 by Washington Yu Ying PCS™

All rights reserved. No part of this book in whole or part may be reproduced without written permission from the publisher.

Published by Level Learning, INC.

Content Contributors:
Washington Yu Ying PCS™
Level Learning - Ya-Ching Chang

Illustrations by: Matt Austin

Leveling classification based on Level Learning standard. For full description, visit www.levellearning.com

ISBN 978-1-64040-008-5
Simplified Chinese Edition

About Level Learning:
Level Learning provides a literacy focused curriculum specifically designed for K-12 Chinese as a Second Language classrooms. Our program offers 20 levels of specific and detailed objectives, leveled texts and passages, mastery-based online assessment, and analytics to enable data-driven instruction. Level Learning reading curriculum for both literature and informational text emphasize grammar and comprehension skills to help teachers develop confident and independent Chinese language readers. The non-fiction series of books are specifically designed to support our informational text course based on multiple national standards. To learn more about our entire offering, visit www.levellearning.com.

About Washington Yu Ying PCS™:
Washington Yu Ying PCS is a Mandarin English dual language immersion International Baccalaureate (IB) World school. Yu Ying's mission is to inspire and prepare young people to create a better world by challenging them to reach their full potential in a nurturing Chinese/English educational environment. Yu Ying's comprehensive IB, dual immersion curriculum equips students with global competencies for success in the real world. As a leader in immersion education, Yu Ying is determined to advance Chinese language programs and global citizenry education by helping other schools create and strengthen their Chinese programs. For more information, email: products@washingtonyuying.org

孔子，出生于公元前551年，春秋时期人。孔子是中国古代著名的思想家，大家又称他为"孔夫子"。孔子的思想流传了两千多年，直到现在，他的思想对中国还是非常重要。

在孔子的思想里,他认为家庭是学习做人最重要的地方。在一个好的家庭里,父母爱孩子,孩子爱父母,兄弟姐妹也相亲相爱。因为家人之间有爱,我们才能学会做人,知道爱别人。因为家人之间有爱,我们就知道要孝敬父母,也知道要尊敬师长。

孔子认为，如果每个人都可以爱别人，就像爱自己的家人一样，这个世界就会更美好。所以，孔子希望人们不要把自己不喜欢的东西或事情，强加在别人身上。

孔子爱人的思想，让他成为一位很好的老师。在中国古代，只有有钱的人才可以去学校学习。但是孔子认为只要是想学习的人，他都应该教他们。孔子一共有三千多个学生。

孔子知道每个人的学习**方法**都不一样,所以他会用不同的方法教学生。即使学生们问孔子一个相同的问题,孔子给每个人的回答都不同。

虽然孔子是老师，但是孔子还是经常向不同的人学习。孔子认为每个人都有自己最**擅长**的事情，每个人都有可以让别人学习的地方。孔子说每三个人里，就有一个人可以做他的老师。

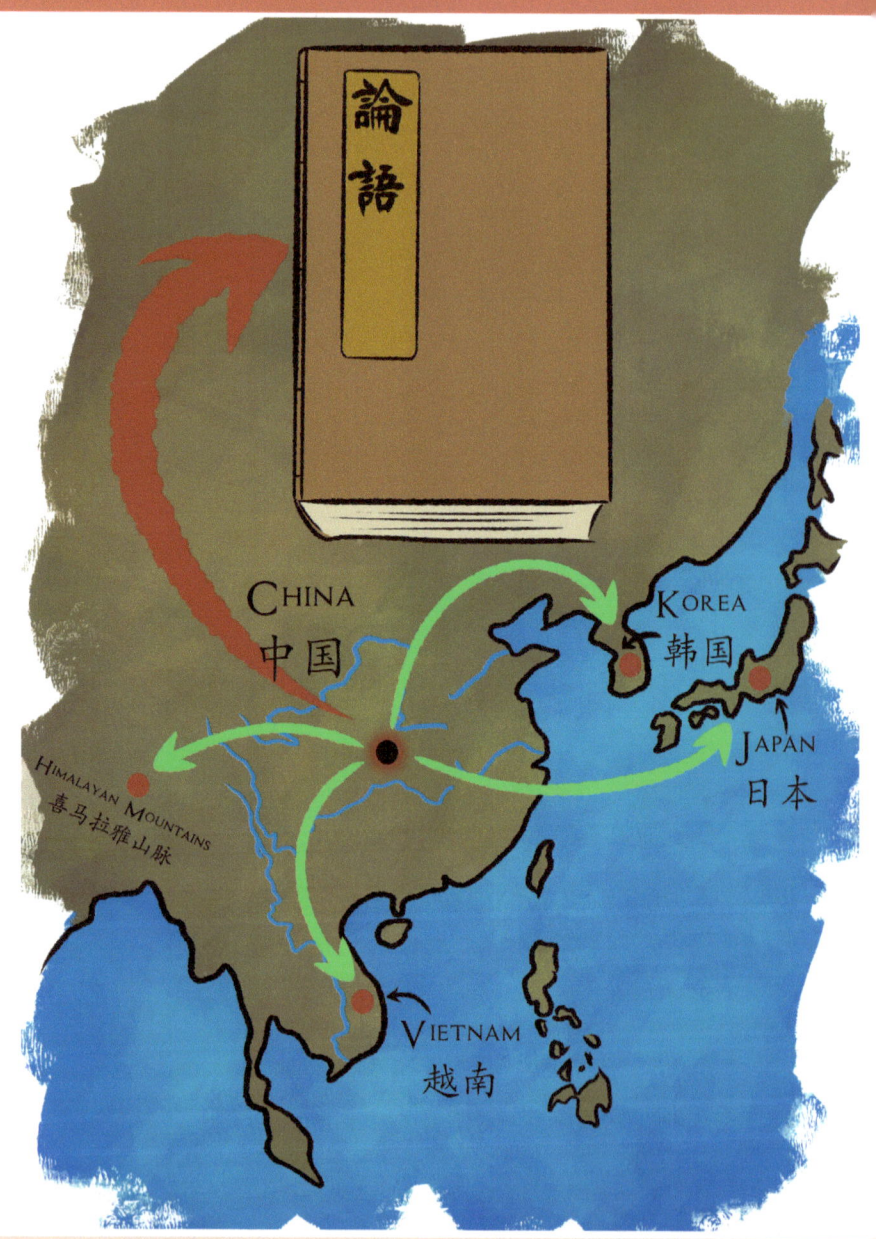

孔子的思想和他说过的话，被他的学生们写成一本书，叫做《论语》。孔子的思想不但在中国有很大的影响，而且还流传到了亚洲其他国家。直到现在，人们的生活还深受孔子思想的影响。

Glossary

	Pinyin	English Definition
公元前	gōng yuán qián	B.C.
时期	shí qī	period
古代	gǔ dài	ancient
著名	zhù míng	famous
思想家	sī xiǎng jiā	thinker, philosopher
思想	sī xiǎng	thinking
流传	liú chuán	to spread
直到	zhí dào	until
重要	zhòng yào	important
认为	rèn wéi	to think
家庭	jiā tíng	family
学习	xué xí	to learn
做人	zuò rén	how to conduct oneself
相亲相爱	xiāng qīn xiāng ài	love each other

	Pinyin	English Definition
孝敬	xiào jìng	to respect and love your parents
尊敬	zūn jìng	to respect
师长	shī zhǎng	teacher
有钱	yǒu qián	rich
教	jiāo	to teach
方法	fāng fǎ	method
擅长	shàn cháng	good at
影响	yǐng xiǎng	influence
亚洲	yà zhōu	Asia

www.ingramcontent.com/pod-product-compliance
Lightning Source LLC
Chambersburg PA
CBHW041225070526
44584CB00001B/106